YOU
VS
YOU

(Fire up your strength, your purpose, and your
motivation)

BY

DOUGLAS WRIGHT

TABLE OF CONTENT

INTRODUCTION

Let's face it, You are reading this book for a purpose. It's because, at least in part, you desire to change. You might not like how mental illnesses affect your daily life, or you might desire to get past the trauma. Maybe you need some tips on how to set yourself up for maximum productivity. Or perhaps you want to work toward a seemingly impossible task that, if successful, will fundamentally alter the direction of your life.

All change is in your hands.
Simply wanting a change is insufficient; you must also act. Just one step in a lifelong journey, reading this book is merely the first step of a lifelong adventure. Every step must be taken by you since no one else will.

No one will go above and beyond for you outside a few extremely close family members and friends. Everyone has their own lives, problems, and obligations to attend to, so while they may offer assistance, it is frequently fairly restricted.

You would be placing yourself in a position of dependence on that individual even if they did provide a significant amount of help. There aren't many partnerships where this is acceptable.

You are relying on someone else if you depend on them. Your ability to grow is therefore constrained by what they do. This will eventually lead to disaster because no one will always be there for you. People change, move, progress, or die. Relationships and enterprises come to an end.

You are the one person who is guaranteed to be there for you for the rest of your life.

Even if people assist you, you must accept it. Someone may have paid for your gym membership, but you must be the one to lift the weights. You may have the help of a therapist, but you must follow their instructions.

You are still the key, regardless of how much attention others are ready to give you.

Don't get me wrong: people care about you and other people.
Every day, kind deeds by people are performed. However, most of these acts can only be carried out by people who are stable enough to not give their lives in the process.

TAKE ACTION

Consider everyone you know. Take into account each person's particular present-day challenges in life.

You will undoubtedly discover that the majority, if not all, have some sort of problem they are dealing with: moving

homes, changing employment, mental illness, accident, disability, relationship challenges, financial difficulties, family dramas, pregnancy, death, etc.
Consider all of it as you respond to the following query:
How much actual assistance have you given them?

The aforementioned TAKE ACTION aims to emphasize exactly how many things are happening at once in your own little space. This, of course, ignores the numerous issues that plague the billions of people living in every corner of the globe, such as poverty, war, displacement, corruption, and the like.

Instead of trying to make you feel guilty, I want to emphasize that it is ultimately up to you to deal with the issues in your life. People are willing to help one another, but the gap between how much is required and how it might be provided is insurmountable.

We have to be accountable for our own life.

Have you ever thought that everything would be wonderful if only someone would provide you with the ideal opportunity or job? Wouldn't it be convenient if all of these items were presented to you at once?
If that were the case, life would be so simple and painless, and isn't that how life should be? Shouldn't we just get everything we ask for handed to us?
Guess what, though?

That is not how life functions.

The only person who can alter your life is you

CHAPTER 1

TAKE CHARGE OF YOUR LIFE.

Whether you like it or not, your happiness and success are entirely your responsibility.

You are living life on your terms if you are the Boss of your life. Unfortunately, a lot of people renounce this opportunity and let their life take a backseat. Take a step back and ask, "Would you pay YOU to run your life?" If not, a change needs to be made.

The world needs you, so be a badass, have faith in your abilities, and take charge of your future. "Your example is the most effective leadership tool you have." Are you prepared to take charge of your life as its CEO?

YOU DETERMINE YOUR OVERALL SUCCESS AS THE CEO OF YOUR LIFE.

Nobody will wave a magic wand for you and make things happen. You need to take command and demand your results as the CEO of your life. Sometimes, this entails being aware of your ideas. You create your reality, so you should pay attention to how you're feeling. If you believe you can, you can accomplish anything in life.

A lot of people, regrettably, hold self-limiting ideas that prevent them from assuming their authority. Automatically pessimistic thoughts These negative, reactionary thoughts are what they sound like. You need to assert yourself when your inner critic rears her ugly head. Why? Since you are in charge of your life, you should always know how to successfully control your emotions.

Here are three strategies for redesigning your "life brand" and letting life know who's in charge:

1. Take ownership of your life.

Being the CEO of your life entails accepting responsibility for all of life's events, both positive and negative. Nobody is to be held accountable for your circumstances. You are the only thing you can control, along with your emotional responses.

Things happen. How do you handle it? Playing the victim and blaming everything around you, or standing up, taking responsibility, and making changes? It's simple to believe that our circumstances or someone else are to blame for preventing us from living the life we desire, yet this is hardly the case.

Become committed to accepting accountability for your life and your choices. According to research, when people make a commitment, their desire to appear "constant" motivates them to carry out their word. You weren't made to be average. Instead, you were destined to shine.

2. Establish A Life Vision

You need a vision for your life, much like a CEO of a company acts according to a vision and mission. Finding out what is essential to you is the first step. How can you expect to ever get to your destination if you don't have a map of where you want to go in life? When life weighs you down, you need something that will help brighten your life course.

If you have a clear vision for your future, you have a far higher chance of success. I implore you to create a life vision statement. What do you want? How would your perfect existence be structured? What kind of impact do you want to have on the world?

Get very clear about the future you desire, and then begin taking steps to make your goals a reality. The purpose of life is to develop oneself, hence, in the words of Robert H. Schuller, "What would you do if you knew you couldn't fail?" Dream enormously large. Too little time remains to not.

3. Ask empowering questions to yourself

How you answer questions can greatly influence how you live your life. Asking empowering questions to yourself is your responsibility as the CEO of your life since doing so allows for countless possibilities and chances for you to grow.

What you pay attention to becomes your reality. You may instantly begin building the route to leading a more resilient life when you teach your brain to concentrate on possibilities and solutions and ask yourself questions such as, "Why is my life so amazing?" or "What am I glad for today?"

Are you prepared to take charge of your life as its CEO?
Keep your life from being controlled by others. Stay away from the leader, Instead, take charge. Pave your way and leave sparkling traces in your wake. Take responsibility and follow your path with passion, tenacity, and persistence because the world needs you to.
"Your example is the most effective leadership tool you have." Are you prepared to take charge, realize your full potential, and exercise your power?

CHAPTER 2

Discover your superpower

Superpowers are frequently misunderstood to be something that only belongs to our favorite superhero characters from comic books or movies. What if I told you that you have superpowers of your own, but it's up to you to find them and put them to good use? Your journey is special, and if you are aware of the superpowers you have, you may navigate it with greater ease and delight.

Superheroes are a subject of intense intrigue in our day and age. The list includes characters like Superman, Batman, Wonder Woman, Wolverine, Spider-Man, Storm, The Incredible Hulk, and many more.

The Best Way To Find Your Superpowers

Is it just a coincidence that superhero movies are breaking box office records? Superheroes are a subject of intense intrigue in our day and age. The list includes characters like Superman, Batman, Wonder Woman, Wolverine, Spider-Man, Storm, The Incredible Hulk, and many more.

What, then, is it about these characters that captivate so many people?

You will learn that you, yes you, have superpowers beyond what you can ever conceive as a result of the response to this question.

Superheroes are beings with immense potential; they are never "born" to be superheroes. The circumstances they find themselves in, the difficulties they encounter, and ultimately the choices they make shape who they become and how they are perceived by others.

More than ever, we identify with superheroes because they have many of the same characteristics as ourselves.

Heroes step up every day to offer their abilities and make a difference in a world where there is so much change, danger, and opportunity for good.

Many real-life superheroes are heroic men and women who have defied all odds to display their special abilities. We can relate to them and the superheroes from the movies because we are all capable of greatness. And in our hearts, we know that we are capable of doing something extraordinary if we are given the proper circumstances, training, and opportunities to "flesh out" our abilities and talents.

If only we were given the chance. If only we knew how to go...

In the recent blockbuster The Man of Steel, young Clark Kent, who portrays many individuals today, had no idea what he was meant to do with his life or what his purpose was. Only by experiencing life, making errors, and learning from them did Clark finally understand what his actual calling was. As a result of everything he endured, he eventually developed into the "Superman" who contributed so much to the world.

There are numerous instances of ordinary people turning into superheroes. I've discovered
The Five Steps to Discovering Your Superpowers, which I'm going to share with you. You can discover your special gifts and talents as well as your ultimate purpose by following these 5 Steps.

Discovering Your Superpowers in 5 Easy Steps

Step 1:
Continuously seek opportunities to grow.

Life is your training field for discovering and honing your inner talents.

Without resistance, it is impossible to get stronger, quicker, better, or more capable. Your special abilities and gifts grow in power just like a muscle. Your results will be better the more resistance you face and exposure you receive.

The difficulties you encounter in life are not intended to weaken you and cause you to give up. They are there to help you grow into the person you need to be to reach your maximum potential.

Everything hinges on your point of view. The choice is yours as to whether you will take the opportunity to grow as a result of your hardships. You have the choice to ignore the situation, refuse to take the lesson and keep making the same error time and time again.

Bottom line: You have a choice.

Be present and wise enough to realize that the obstacles you confront are opportunities waiting to be seized. You can only discover how amazing you are by looking for these opportunities and being prepared for them.

Step 2:
Face your concerns -
Why would someone turn out the chance to grow from their struggles and ultimately improve themselves? They are terrified, is the clear-cut response. It's not a problem that we are all built to fear the unknown. It has a purpose since it keeps us safe, so that's for sure. However, if we don't see past the fear and let it rule our lives, this hard-wiring may severely

destroy us and prevent us from moving forward.

Note that I stated "permit." This is because fear is a natural response, but it is entirely up to you how you handle it.

For instance, if someone has an "incurable" sickness, they can hesitate to take action out of concern that they won't recover. There are currently too many examples of people surviving terminal illnesses to list them all. The distinction for them is that they decided to resist accepting the label that someone else had placed on them. Instead, they decided to confront their anxiety head-on, take action, and let the cards fall as they might. They came to the key realization that giving up is the only surefire way to fail.

Some typical worries that people have overcome to achieve their ultimate brilliance include the following:
*Fear of being rejected

*The fear of failing

*Worry about what other people will say

*Afraid of dying (from a terminal illness to dangerous feats of courage)

*Worry over not being sufficient

"With every event where you truly stop to face fear, you get stronger, braver, and more self-assured. You must take the action that you believe you cannot take. Being great requires overcoming your fears. No matter where they are in life, every superhero has fears. So keep in mind that while fear may occasionally surface, it is always up to you how you respond to it.

Step 3:
Go with your gut - If you knew you couldn't fail, what would you do with your life? What would you be doing with your life if you had the true choice if you were to look within yourself honestly?

You DO have a choice.

Following one's genuine calling is one of the most daring things one can do, despite what it may sound like. We frequently unwittingly follow social norms that have been established as being righteous, respectable, or "safe" for us to follow. Many people put their interests on the back burner to conform to what society expects of them.

It's important to consider your friends, family, and teachers' opinions. But this is YOUR life, and you have the chance to make it extraordinary.

You alone have special abilities and gifts that no one else possesses. You are the only person like you, and you will always be the only one.

You have the right—in some ways even the duty—to develop your special talents and make them known to the rest of the world. Because they choose to follow their hearts, so many people have altered the trajectory of human history. The world would be much darker today if Thomas Edison had listened to the doubters and those who felt they were assisting him by advising him to give up (literally).

The great historical personalities all over the world overcame hardship and frequently accomplished things that had never been done before. Just because something hasn't been done before (within your circle of friends, family, or the entire planet), doesn't imply it can't be done. It only needs your willingness to make it happen.

We are a part of history at an amazing time. It's a moment when investing in your passions and following your heart may help you both make a difference and support yourself.

Being responsible is one thing, but giving up your goals is quite another. The cosmos works with you to fulfill your mission, according to many wise teachings. But it requires action on your part to accept it and start moving boldly in that direction.

Step 4:
Ask powerful questions. The human mind is wired so that it MUST look for solutions to the problems it is presented with.

Our intellect is automatically focused on questions. Finding the answers you're seeking will be easier if you ask the correct questions.

The main problem is that most individuals use the power we all possess carelessly. They frequently pose dehumanizing queries like:

*Why me?

*What's the matter with me?

Why won't anyone come to my aid?

*Why am I unable to get a break?

*Why does this keep happening to me?

Your brain automatically looks for information to aid in providing answers to these queries. You, why? Below is a list. What's the matter with you? Below is a list.

You'll keep coming up with more "why you"s and be preoccupied with your shortcomings rather than your potential greatness.

The easiest method to alter a response is to ask the proper question. Start asking questions that are helpful to you and propel you ahead rather than backward if you want to become empowered in your mind, body, and soul. Try these questions instead when you're in a difficult scenario or just unsure circumstances:

*What about this is right?

What current skills or abilities do I have that might be useful in this?

*How am I going to enjoy doing this?

*What do I need to take away from this?

*Where is the blessing or gift in this?

*What traits are these causing me to desire to develop?

You may alter the way your mind works by asking empowering questions. Although it takes practice, there are several advantages along the road. You must concentrate on finding solutions rather than problems if you want to realize your heroic potential. Discover the solutions you require to carry out your purpose for being on the planet by using the power of your thoughts.

Step 5:

Be Ready: The road to greatness is not always easy to travel. You'll need to overcome challenges, build strength and skills, safeguard yourself from hardship, and make difficult choices when everything is at stake.

The superhero's desire to go the extra mile in his or her greatest strength. Superheroes are ready to set an example, stand up for what they believe in, and never give up.

Usually, the going is difficult at first. Trying to follow your aspirations when you decide to break the mold can frequently feel like an uphill battle. But rest assured that if you persevere and adhere to the instructions given here, you will succeed and the going gets a lot simpler from there.

Your life's difficulties exist to help qualify you for success. If you didn't have to strive for your success, you wouldn't recognize or realize its importance. Always keep in mind that the real prize isn't what you obtain, but rather who you grow to be along the way.

So, whatever your special mission is, be prepared to accept it. You have the potential to affect global change because "great power comes with tremendous responsibility."

Chapter 3

What motivates you?

I'm doing this, but why? When we challenge ourselves to do something or reach a goal, we probably ask ourselves this question rather frequently. The secret to our success is in the actual response to that question. However, we don't just want the quick, cursory response. We must discover the fundamental explanation, the underlying cause of why you wake up in the morning.

Knowing your "why" will be essential to attaining all of your goals in life, including those related to your health and fitness. Every time things get difficult if you are aware of your "why," you will turn to it and find the strength and determination to press on.
Your mission, identity, cause, principles, or beliefs make up your WHY. It is the

reason behind your actions, and this is true for both private persons (like you) and corporate entities.

Purpose

Your objectives and desires might be connected to your distinct sense of purpose in life. You are more likely to succeed in achieving your objectives and desires if you tie them to your true purpose, or "why," since they will have a deeper significance.

Finding your purpose might be challenging for some people, and it differs for each person. One person's goal may be to take care of people, another person's goal may be to raise a lot of money for charity, and yet another person's goal may be to protect the environment.

When you finally understand why you were born, it's like a light bulb moment. It is the instant when everything suddenly makes sense. You prioritize this one thing above all others, which demonstrates how willing you are to do everything it takes to achieve it. It can hit you like a bolt of lightning or it might be something you discover after some introspection.

When you know what your mission is, you have something to hold onto when things got difficult. You are more likely to find the strength to continue if your purpose is rooted in pleasant emotions since it is more deeply ingrained than a surface-level aim. However, this is not to say that what might initially seem to be a "superficial" goal won't have some profoundly ingrained emotional link; you only need to delve a little farther to uncover the true motivation behind your desire.

I've said it so many times before, but my goal is always to set a good example for my kids, to be the best mother I can be, and to make sure they have strong, healthy bodies as youngsters. I wasn't particularly aware of it until I joined Be Strong with Rick and started to seriously consider why I became more physically active, healthier, and lighter...Everything was automatic. But now that I've identified and defined my purpose, it unquestionably motivates me to move forward in all I do. I believe that having recognized that has given me greater motivation to carry on and continue doing what I am doing since everything I do has a connection. It motivates me to strive to be the best version of myself that I can be. That's not to say I don't stumble periodically; after all, we are all only human. But when I stumble, it gives me the motivation to get back up.

You find your most potent source of inspiration when you are connected to your actual mission. It motivates you to get out of bed each morning. It offers you courage when things are difficult and a cause to get yourself back up when you fall off the wagon.

Why should I discover my purpose?

A goal is not your purpose. It is an emotionally driven motivation with profound roots. You may stay focused and devoted to attaining your goals by discovering your purpose and keeping it in mind.

Finding your purpose encourages you to cease engaging in aspects of your former way of life that you know you should but don't truly want to. The motivation to quit purchasing garbage at the store "for the kids/guests/husband/dog/neighbors' aunties' sister-in-law" when you want it comes from knowing what you want. It makes the new way of life more desirable than the old way of existence. It motivates you to want to do this enough to give up your old, harmful habits to achieve your goals.

Finding your purpose could completely change your life. The boundary between the old and the new may be marked by this line in the sand. When you know why you're here, it inspires and motivates you to start acting now and stay acting forever. This will continue until the day we die, and if we stop, we just return to where we were, so it won't be until you reach a certain weight on the scales, climb that mountain, or get rid of those crutches.

How can I discover my purpose?

You must set aside some time to uncover your purpose, usually between 10 and 15 minutes without any other distractions. Only then will you be able to think clearly and concentrate on what you truly desire.

You must first determine what your interim aim is. The objective should be defined so that you can track your development from where you are now to where you want to finish. As a result, that could be: "I wish to be 11 stones."

Then, you must ask yourself why you want to weigh 11 stones. For each reason you offer yourself, you must then question yourself why. Asking more whys will help you understand yourself better and get closer to your purpose. When we keep asking ourselves these questions, it can get pretty uncomfortable, but don't be afraid of the answers because when you discover the answers, then is when magic can begin to happen.

Your objective may not be to lose weight but rather to improve your physical capabilities, such as "I want to climb the tallest mountain in England" or "I want to be able to walk without a cane." The road continues to be the same, so why? Keep asking yourself why until you discover the real, profound answer; this is what you need to do.

Finding your purpose may require you to engage in some serious soul-searching and introspection, something you may not have had the time or the comfort to do in the past. But the magic will begin to work once you discover your purpose. Your goal will offer you motivation to keep on track or, if you fall off, to pick yourself back up quickly.

Flip it on its head if the responses to your queries are unfavorable or focused on unfavorable emotions. If your response was, "I don't want to be the person who doesn't achieve things anymore," try flipping it to, "I want to be the one that everyone thinks will achieve what they say they will." I aspire to be the hero that everyone looks up to. When you need to fall back on it to motivate yourself to keep going or get yourself back up, it is far more inspiring and powerful. When you stumble, if you are focused on a bad goal, you will likely just give up and that goal will come true. However, if your goal is positive, then just reflecting on that goal will give you the energy and the willpower to get back up and keep going.

Put your objective in writing and post it somewhere you'll see it every day. A regular reminder will give you the focus you need to continue, whether it's written in the steam on the bathroom mirror, your screen saver on your phone, or on your computer at work.

CHAPTER 4

WORK TOWARD YOUR PURPOSE

Significance is more important than motivation when it comes to purpose. Even if you weren't required to, you would still be doing it. You can feel content without needing the earnings from it.

Status is not necessary: The impact is more important than the image here. After a challenging day or encounter, it's what gives you life again. It is what motivates you. It is your "why." It involves more than merely checking things off a list of to-dos or accomplishing goals. It's what makes you happy. And it concerns what you would do if fear were not a factor.

Each person's perception of who they are and what they want to do determines how their purpose is defined. It can be achieving something, loving someone, telling your story, standing up for something, getting beyond a challenge, and more. It can be reinterpreted as many times as necessary. It's never too late to make a fresh start or begin living on purpose.

Align Your Thoughts And Actions With Your Goal

Imagine yourself living your purpose, just as you want to.

Add as many details as you can. How do you feel?

What do you think about this?

What are the costs associated with getting there? How is life different from how it is right now?

Don't stress about getting from point A to point B. It makes no difference how.

You'll come up with a solution. You'll rely on your "why."

Focus intensely on your routines:

Get up each day prepared to work for it because it won't just happen to you. You must want it more than everyone else. With this outlook, momentum will increase.

Avoid concentrating on your shortcomings or inner critic:
 Don't think about what you've lost. Rejections shouldn't be your main focus because they are a natural part of life. As you pursue your dreams, pay attention to the thoughts you choose to think. Start seeing the possibilities rather than the impossibilities.
Keep being original throughout. Push on even if you are the only person on your road. You might be clearing the way for someone else. You may be the only person doing what you're doing, and there's a good reason for that. You should be genuine in your accomplishments.

Concentrate on your Strengths
Are all of your efforts yielding the desired results?
If not, perhaps it's time to consider the following:

Do you have the proper priorities in mind?
Do you have a lack of attention and energy? Arc you aware of your strong points?
I've learned a lot over the years, including the fact that focusing on too many things at once will prevent you from getting the best outcomes. However, even more, crucial than that is to make sure your attention is on what you do best because this is when you will produce your finest work and outcomes.

Why is it crucial to concentrate on your strong Strength?
You must fight the tendency to concentrate on your weaknesses and begin leveraging your strengths if you want to succeed.

However, a lot of us spend too much time criticizing ourselves and giving ourselves constructive criticism. A paradigm shift is necessary. Only thinking about our weaknesses leads to further weakness. Finding fault constantly is not a productive self-improvement tactic. A person must be aware of their strengths and apply them for the larger good to be truly happy and lead a meaningful life.

If we are to heed this advice, we should take the time to identify our unique skills rather than squandering our time and lives on tasks that don't fulfill us and keep us from accomplishing what we were created to do. If this is the key to happiness, then we should all be concentrating on what we are good at and not waste time on the rest.

Pareto principle

The Pareto Principle demonstrates how narrowing your focus can lead to greater success. The Pareto Principle, sometimes known as the 80/20 rule, is a widely accepted theory that holds in many areas of life. Sales leaders utilize it to determine who their key clients are. They are aware that 20% of their clients and 20% of their products will generate 80% of their revenue for them. The astute understand that after identifying that 20%, they should concentrate their efforts there. Results will be attained more quickly and efficiently with this approach.

Your bank account will benefit if you devote the majority of your time and effort to crucial clients. Your current good clients will develop into exceptional ones. Imagine the outcomes if you applied this idea to every aspect of your life and concentrated only on your strengths. If you stopped doing the tasks that don't bring value or that another person could complete for you. This will undoubtedly help you achieve your goals more quickly because you can focus all of your energy on your strengths.

How to Use Your Strength.

Working smarter is the key to success.
Here are 5 options for you:

1. Identify your goals and the things you wish to accomplish to chart your course.
You've always had a sense of adventure. You decide that, within the following year, you want to leave your 9 to 5 job and start your own business.

2. Consider how your strengths can assist you in achieving your goals:
SWOT analysis should be done.
Your SWOT analysis' strengths definitions might act as a roadmap for your future.
Maybe you have a knack for working with metal. You decide to start a business creating metal art after doing some research. You make the decision that you want to save up enough money within the next six months to quit your job and work as a blacksmith full-time.

3. Put your attention on the talents you need to develop to play to your strengths.
Focus most of your focus on honing your strengths rather than worrying about the things you don't do well.

You'll need to acquire new skills to launch your own metalworking company. You'll need to determine where to obtain the supplies you need for this kind of work, as well as how to develop a clientele. You'll need to spend some time networking in addition to honing your metalworking skills. You must take all of these actions to afford to develop your metalworking abilities.

4. You can run into challenges along the way, and that's when you'll realize which areas need improvement.
You should take immediate action to address any weaknesses that are impeding your capacity to accomplish your goals. You could achieve this by learning new

skill sets or locating a coworker who excels in a field that challenges you.

Imagine that you have to file quarterly taxes since your company is doing so well. You object to this because you don't know how the tax system works. You employ a CPA rather than wasting time on taxes when you could be using that time to create magnificent sculptures with your specific knowledge. The CPA has a unique set of specialized talents and knows how to ensure that you abide by tax regulations and receive the most deductions possible.

5. Keep your attention on developing your advantages.

There are some things that no one else can do as well as you. You can spend time working to improve your best if you can identify what those things are.

You've already mastered one type of metalworking to a high level. You might experiment with other materials or look for a mentor who can show you new approaches to hone your strengths. Being unable to work with some metals in this situation is more like unrealized potential than a handicap.

6. Don't let your shortcomings cause you to drown.

When you focus on the bad, you deny yourself the chance to succeed. You can achieve success more quickly by developing an asset-based mindset and understanding your strengths. Focus on maximizing your abilities rather than wandering down rabbit holes to take on work that requires a specialist or beating yourself up over immutable features of your character. You'll not only be happy, but you'll also be more successful.

Positivity Is The Key To Success And Happiness

When you focus on the bad, you deny yourself the chance to succeed. You can achieve success more quickly by developing an asset-based mindset and understanding your strengths. Focus on maximizing your abilities rather than wandering down rabbit holes to take on work that requires a specialist or beating yourself up over immutable features of your character. You'll not only be happy, but you'll also be more successful.

The new productivity is happiness. Everything you do will have an even greater impact if you're in a flowing mood or are creative. While having goals is necessary, your happiness shouldn't be dependent on them. You must be content right now. If you are not satisfied with what you are doing, you will never achieve your greatest success. Do what makes you joyful, and you'll induce a state of flow that will lead to your success forever.

Spend some time discovering your strengths and what activities bring you into flow if you haven't previously. When you are aware of the action, give it your full attention and effort. You should "only do what only you can do," concentrate on 20% of the work and delegate 80% of the work that you don't need to do to others. Not only will you become more effective, creative, and productive by doing this, but you'll also become happier and more successful.

Review and reevaluate your goal

Be conscious that as you mature and develop your knowledge, your life's purpose may change. You can have your sights set on one item in the beginning but end up with something quite different. You might take your focus off of what you're doing right now. There might be a detour. None of these things interfere with your destiny. In actuality, finding meaning involves being adaptable. Be flexible with your purpose when you decide on it. It could change over time depending on how you define it. Your original objective might be abandoned if you see and do more.

Have you taken any actions that have an impact? Other than your own, have you made a difference in anyone else's life? Have you persevered despite having every desire to give up? Have you managed to stay motivated by your "why"?

Change it if it isn't working, That's completely ok. That does not imply that you are a failure. It just suggests that you should try a different tactic or look for a new project to inspire you to complete your aim. It simply signifies that the door closing wasn't the best choice for you. However, you shouldn't let that stop you from knocking. The appropriate door will ultimately open, and you'll see that it was all worthwhile.

Conclusion: Living with Purpose
Living with purpose entails remembering your starting point or evaluating your "why"; it also entails matching your thoughts and actions with your purpose

and periodically examining and reevaluating them. Your calling will then become immediately apparent when you do. And you live in a way that will be revered and remembered. You make decisions about your future and are aware of your value. Most importantly, you make the necessary preparations to make it happen. No matter the detour, you produce good along the route. And even if you shift course, you do so consciously. Change the world, and you will change.

Then and only then can you declare that you lived intentionally.

CHAPTER 5

KNOWLEDGE IS THE NEW CURRENCY

Nowadays, the majority of people have the problem of prioritizing material wealth over intellectual curiosity. They spend so much time pursuing money that they fail to understand that knowledge is the new kind of currency.

We should question ourselves, "Why do the world's smartest and busiest people find one hour a day for deliberate study, while others make excuses about how busy they are?"

What do they notice that others don't? The simple response is that investing time in education is the best use of our time. Today, ignorance makes you poor and knowledge makes you rich. Your knowledge is now the new currency in this brave new world. Knowledge is becoming more valuable in a world where goods and services are demonetizing. Few individuals are aware of this realization, but it is essential for success in our knowledge economy.

Knowledge is a powerful thing! The new currency that can enable you to participate in the dialogue of today and the future is knowledge. What do you have in your "knowledge wallet" then? Although you don't have to be an expert, it is crucial to comprehend the new knowledge language. Don't pass up the chance to educate yourself about subjects that are relevant to your field of study or employment at your own pace. Everything in existence is based on knowledge. Without knowledge, nothing would be as we understand it to be. It is essential. Any foundation is built on knowledge. The secret to unlocking locked doors is knowledge. Only because people are aware and knowledgeable are commodities sought after.

Learning is one of the most significant things we can do in our life. Everyone likes to learn, even if we didn't like school or had anxiety before exams. Humans are curious by nature. Just because school is ended doesn't imply you've learned everything and can stop learning. On the contrary, the school only provided you with some useful knowledge and the means to continue learning throughout the rest of your life.

That's a big task, and with so many opportunities and solutions available, it could be difficult to know where to start.

LEARN A SKILL

One of the most gratifying things you can do to advance is to learn a new skill. Learning a new skill is not only a wise financial move, but it is also beneficial to your mental well-being. You feel more strong when you acquire new skills. When you learn anything new, your brain creates new neural connections. Changing your mind is the best approach to improving your life. And the easiest way to change your viewpoint is by picking up new talents.

When your life becomes monotonous due to your daily routine, amusement is insufficient to reenergize you. Weekend entertainment can be enjoyable, but if you don't learn anything new for years, you'll begin to despise your job.

According to the conventional educational model, we are expected to complete high school and college before beginning a career. That approach might have been successful thirty years ago when the world was gradually transitioning into the information age. It won't function any longer. Learning must become a habit, and skills must be continuously updated to remain relevant and competitive in today's world.

After high school and college, studying becomes a solitary endeavor, which is one of the toughest hurdles. Learning can be stressful if you're using a book or an online course with a series of video sessions. When students are enthusiastic and content, they learn best. And the only way to feel upbeat while learning is to associate with a group of people who share your educational objectives.

One thing is obvious when you consider the trends that are influencing how we learn and work. Knowledge is extremely valuable, and the way it is presented, used, and leveraged in the workplace demonstrates that it is the new currency for careers.

Chapter 6

YOU ARE AN ENTERPRISE

What is an enterprise?
The word "enterprise" has many meanings. Human skill: the will to take chances and try something innovative. An individual who possesses this talent is entrepreneurial; he or she is enterprising. He or she is ready to

Take Any risks: Anyone who has started a new business can attest to the risks involved. No matter how thoroughly a market is studied, there is always a chance that clients won't like the product or that another issue will arise, preventing the company from turning a profit.
People "play it safe" far too often. This is where mediocrity plays. Ordinary people reside there. They always follow the rules and stay within the lines. They avoid

going outside the bounds whenever possible out of fear of the unknown. Those who "play it safe" are easy to predict. Rules and rituals govern their way of life. The views of others frequently guide their behavior. This group fights to maintain the status quo.

But risk-takers are a distinct kind. They are surrounded by opportunity and excellence. They don't hesitate to break the rules and express themselves in unconventional ways. They believe that only unsuccessful experiments qualify as failures. Risk-takers exhibit an adventurous and passionate spirit. The acclaim of the audience means little to them. They place a greater emphasis on making the most of each moment. "Boldly go where no one has gone before," they say, without fear.
Consider this. Name one historical individual who, by being safe and typical, made a difference. The majority of accomplished individuals are remembered for the contributions they made during

their lives. They had to take chances and question the status quo because of this discrepancy.

People who push the bounds of what is possible and go above and beyond the norm inspire us. On the other side, mediocrity does not motivate. It also doesn't lead to success. If you aren't willing to push the boundaries that you have set for yourself and that other people have set for you, success, whatever you define it, will elude you.

If the Orville brothers had listened to the doubters, their historic flight might never have taken place. If Henry Ford had listened to his detractors, the vehicle would not have been created. If David had let his own family discourage him, he would have never been able to vanquish Goliath. The list goes on and on.

Every significant development in history—in business, science, medicine, athletics, etc.—came about as a result of a person taking a chance and refusing to play it safe. successful people understand this. Their sense of adventure leads to their ingenuity. They invent because they risk living outside the confines of the standard, accomplishing, surpassing, and succeeding.

Risk-taking is a trait of successful people, but they don't take reckless risks. Only an idiot would rush in. They could appear to others to be acting foolishly, but nothing could be further from the reality. Great people take calculated risks to succeed. They consider their options and reason out their decisions. They do research and get the information they require to decide wisely. The benefits and negatives are weighed.

But after conducting their research, successful people differ from others in that they TAKE ACTION! They leap into action. They dare to advance. They accept the danger!

Make Things Happen: A true entrepreneur is motivated, focused, and driven to tackle the challenges and potential pitfalls that come with starting a new company.

Successful individuals act as a spark. They bring about events. They are resolved to act and change the world because they are passionate and inspired by their dreams. They are not content to do nothing or put off doing something. They spread their zeal and bravery to others. If you hang out with a catalyst like this, eventually you might want to support their cause! That's one of the things I love the most—as a business coach—about spending time with other business owners!

The majority of individuals desire a better future. They have separate worlds in their dreams. But visionaries believe they can change the world. Dreamers imagine how wonderful it would be if somebody did something. Visionaries search for chances to bring their ideas to life. "Good things come to those who wait, but merely the things left over by those who hustle," as Abraham Lincoln famously stated, Both your personal and professional lives are goals of yours. Do something now; don't wait for inspiration! There are never ideal circumstances. People who wait till all conditions are favorable don't take any action. They put off doing things repeatedly, and as a result, their fantasies never come true. They frequently experience anxiety and self-doubt. You must behave as though you expect to reach the end zone if you want to accomplish your professional or personal goals. Do not wait for events to occur. Make them happen and stand out from the crowd.

Try Something New: How do you stay excited about life? The most crucial thing you can do, in my opinion, is to create opportunities for yourself rather than just take advantage of them when they arise. Consider the activities on your "bucket list" that you've always wanted to try. Why are you holding out? Why not go out and cross one of those things off your list today? Or maybe you want to act impulsively and try something you've never thought about. You can continue to improve your life as long as you keep trying out new endeavors and pursuits.

An innovative and perceptive individual can spot business prospects that will meet customer demands and close market gaps.

The ability to think creatively is a trait shared by all businesspeople. They take the initiative and come up with fresh ideas.
One who "makes things happen" takes the initiative. He or she frequently takes action. When a business opportunity presents itself, the person seizes it. Being bold and making decisions are traits that not everyone possesses, but the initiative does.

Try new activities and get outside of your comfort zone. You can only develop and find new interests and pastimes if you give them a chance. But whatever the outcome, accept it and go on. If you attempt something and it turns out to not be your thing, that's cool. You at least gave it a try. There is no need to continue doing it. Simply move on to the next thing that grabs your attention.

CHAPTER 7

BE INTENTIONAL

Being intentional implies being able to envision certain outcomes in the future that, if attained, will lead to better and bigger things in your life, your business, and yourself.

A devoted, purposeful, and deliberate manner of thinking about your business and life is called having an intentional focus. When you make decisions and take action on what is important to you, you are being purposeful. Being deliberate is being forthright and transparent about your goals.

You consciously decide to pursue a particular end or result in the future that is significant to you. This might be something you wish to have in your life or a goal you want to accomplish.

Then, you take daily action to work toward reaching the desired result or conclusion. By being deliberate, you may concentrate more on your priorities.

By deciding to act on the things that are significant to you, you can learn to be more intentional. Living with intention entails making deliberate decisions to live the life you desire rather than letting other people control your thoughts, feelings, and behavior.

If you're an intentional person, everything you do has a specific goal in mind. When you are intentional, you don't allow fear to hold you back; instead, you concentrate your time and efforts on your assets and the positive aspects of your life.

Intentional people are action-oriented, unwavering in their resolve, and committed to achieving their goals. It's crucial to be self-aware, to say no more often than you say yes, and to cultivate thankfulness if you want to become more intentional.

With intention, you can cultivate gratitude for the things that are most important in your life and increase your appreciation for them. When you build stronger boundaries around your time and the key areas of your life, you are being deliberate.

When you are deliberate, abundance is your main priority. Learn how to adopt an abundant attitude by reading my guide.

WHY LIVE WITH INTENT?

A way of life known as intentional living pushes us to establish our priorities, become crystal clear on our life goals, and live each day following these priorities.

Living intentionally simply involves determining what you want out of life and pursuing it!

It certainly comes as no surprise that intentional living is growing in acceptance in today's hectic environment when many of us are overworked and juggling "all the things."

We're looking for a life of meaning, direction, clarity, calm, and joy rather than chasing our tails and battling life in the fast lane. a life that is determined by us rather than by our schedule or to-do list.

INTENTIONALITY SKILLS

It doesn't cost money or take a lot of effort to be intentional. It won't require you to give anything up or discard everything, unless you choose to, of course!

Making modest, deliberate judgments each day about what improves your life and what only clutters, distracts, and deviates from your goals is what it means to live intentionally. These little choices add up to create a greater image of your life.

Making our own decisions before letting other people's decisions define us is the art of intentional living.

If leading an intentional life resonates with you, this book might offer some straightforward tips for doing so every day. We'll look at some doable advice that will assist you in building a life that is more in line with your preferences.

I hope you find these suggestions useful in building a life that supports you (instead of just exhausting you!) whether it's being purposeful with your time, relationships, self-care, finances, priorities, or anything else that makes up your life.

BEGINNING TO ACT WITH INTENTION

I didn't start decluttering and simplifying my life intentionally when I initially started doing it for myself. I had no idea what intentional living even entailed!

I simply knew that my busy home and busy life were overtaxing both my body and mind. Life was pushing and pulling me in numerous directions, and I felt like I was straying from my path more and more.

I had forgotten what I wanted from life, what meant the most to me, and what gave my life meaning and purpose. In actuality, I was preoccupied with errand running, juggling my children and my job, and snatching sleep and energy snacks whenever I could.

I didn't want my life to be like this, but I also didn't know how to make it different.

Even though I wasn't aware of it at the time, I started being intentional by clearing out clutter and streamlining my life.

I continually made minor, daily judgments about what was and wasn't significant. To protect the things in my life that was far more essential than merely being junk, I got rid of the clutter, kept the stuff out, and set limits.

It wasn't without difficulties, and numerous times I thought I had lost my focus or was "doing it incorrectly." But with time, I realized that my attitude toward living shifted gradually. I started living consciously by making the decisions, choices, deeds, actions, routines, and routines that I followed and followed.

DAILY WAYS TO BE INTENTIONAL

Here are some suggestions for how to practice purpose each day. Examine their effectiveness in practice.

1. Establish a definite schedule for your day.

Establish a reliable and dependable morning and evening schedule for yourself (and your family). No matter how busy you've been in between, having a clear plan for your day can help you start and end it on the correct note.

You can make time for your priorities, your family, and yourself with the help of this organized schedule.

"How you live your life is determined by how you spend your days."

This phrase is a potent reminder that an intentional life begins with an intentional day if you still need more persuading.

However, it does allow you a flexible approach to planning your day and carves out time for what's essential (to you, not your to-do list!). A clear structure doesn't have to be inflexible or prevent you from acting on whims.

2. Take good care of your money:
How simple is it to visit the store when we're
feeling down or if we're bored and have nothing better to do?

Everybody needs to shop occasionally, and buying new items is wonderful. Instead, be deliberate in your expenditures. Avoid wasting money or buying goods you don't need or want because they will only empty your bank account and clog your cabinets.

3. Organize your home.
Although your house is your area, everything in it has a cost. Depending on how much you spent for it initially or how much time and effort you put into caring for it.
Be thoughtful about the things you retain in your house. Get rid of anything you

don't love, need, or that doesn't bring value in any manner. Enjoy living in an area that is free of clutter, easy to maintain clean, and organized, and that gives you more room, time, and energy for other aspects of your life.

4. Identify your objectives and priorities.

How often do you consider your objectives and what you hope to accomplish in life? You could think that your objective as a busy person is simply to get through the day, but there is so much more you can accomplish!

Priorities and objectives aid in providing clarity for our aspirations. They serve as a reminder that despite being a parent, a spouse, and everything else we wear daily, we are still unique individuals.

5. Use your time effectively.

Time is valuable. It's possible to argue that it's both our most finite resource and the one we waste or misuse the most.

Avoid overcommitting, spreading yourself too thin, overbooking or double booking oneself, and saying "yes" to requests when you'd prefer to say "no." Spending your time in a way that is in line with your priorities requires being deliberate with it.

6. Strengthen your crucial connections. It's simple to take our relationships with others for granted when life gets busy. We forget to connect with and prioritize the time spent with the people who are most important to us.

However, for them to be robust, relationships must be worked on. Be deliberate in how you choose your friends. Find strategies to distance yourself from relationships that appear a little one-sided and concentrate on mutually supportive ones. Why not call your parent, schedule coffee with your best friend, have a conversation with your spouse, or spend time with your children after reading this?

7. Develop a positive outlook

Our mindset determines how we view life, the choices and decisions we make, and whether or not we act. Make the most of your life by not letting it pass you by.

To truly embrace an intentional existence, look into techniques for cultivating a good, healthy outlook, and purge mental clutter for greater clarity and focus,

8. Establish wholesome routines

Everyone understands the value of taking care of oneself, staying active, and eating well. But if it's not feasible, you don't have to complete the marathon or even sign up for a gym membership! Instead, simply be conscious of what you put into and how you use your body.

Decide to move more, even if it's only taking the dog or kids for frequent walks. Be mindful of the food you purchase and feed your family. You'll feel better, have more energy, and be able to live a fuller, happier life.

9. Take your mental health seriously

Be intentional and conscious of your emotions and mental condition while keeping your mental health in mind. Consider what caused your feelings of anger, upset, anxiety, or overwhelm as well as how they are affecting you and what you may do to alleviate them.

Don't be scared to accept offers of support and seek assistance. Don't ignore your unfavorable ideas in the hopes that they would disappear. Own them and make an effort to address them.

Writing everything down on paper is a smart first step when you're feeling depressed or out of sorts since it helps you organize and clarify your ideas and create an action plan. After all, living with intention involves taking action in a big way!

10. Taking care of oneself and reflecting

We are so quick to place ourselves last on the list of priorities. Instead, make time for yourself a priority. As a result, you'll become a better, stronger person who is better able to handle the stresses of daily life and is more prepared for new chances as they present themselves.

An excellent method to be deliberate is through self-care and self-reflection. They exhort us to center our attention within rather than on the outside world. While much of our time is spent navigating our external environments, living a meaningful, purposeful life requires attention to what is happening internally, in our inner habitats.

11. Make a plan, get organized, and prepare

Getting organized, in my opinion, genuinely supports living intentionally. It involves more than just getting organized. What matters most is what organizing yourself can do for you.

You may create more time, more peace and ease, more freedom, less stress, and less spinning around in circles if you plan, prepare, and organize your day or life a little. You'll forget less, anticipate and avoid difficulties, and generally feel more in control because you'll know what needs to be done and when.

12. Use social media responsibly.

I occasionally need to distance myself from social media and take a break. I use it for work, my blog, and occasionally for personal use, but there comes a time when I feel like taking a break.

While I enjoy learning about other people's lives, I also enjoy improving my own. Scrolling aimlessly through feeds is not only a huge waste of time, but it's also simple to get seduced by glossy lifestyle photos, smart advertisements, and other photos and messages that make me feel inferior. I don't want to evaluate myself in terms of how I appear to others, how my house appears, or how full my life is.

13. Show gratitude

The secret to living consciously is to be thankful for what we already have rather than chasing after what we don't. We'll never be satisfied if we're constantly looking to the outside world for things that will make us happier, richer, more successful, or anything else that we desire or believe we can't live without. But frequently, we already have a lot of what we require within and all around us. We may better control it by living intentionally and with an attitude of thankfulness.

14. Ignore comparisons and concentrate on your life.

Give up attempting to be something you're not! Focus on your own life and make it the best it can be instead of worrying about what other people are doing with theirs.

CHAPTER 8

YOU VS YOU: The only one against you is you

How many times in your life—or even just one day—have you felt as though the odds are stacked against you? On the way to work, perhaps, you dropped your coffee. Perhaps your child kept you awake all night. Perhaps you are unable to shed those troublesome middle pounds. The majority of the time, anything we struggle with in life feels like it is happening TO us rather than being a random coincidence. The fact of the issue is that everything we experience in life has more to do with how we respond to it than with what has already occurred or is currently occurring. We have the option of letting events alter us negatively or positively. I'd go with option 1, but how about you? After all, what is life if we aren't always trying to be the best versions of ourselves? Why would we deliberately try to make things worse?

The more I mature, the more I understand that life is not all rainbows and fairies. Many difficulties exist in life. Life is unforgiving. However, if we let it, life may still be very joyful. We are impacted in some manner by everything that occurs in our life. We learn to dream big as children and not let obstacles in life get in the way of our goals. Even if this is still sound advice, it isn't the whole story. I'm going to take a moment to paint this picture in broad strokes; please bear with me while I do so. I know that everyone is raised somewhat differently and has quite diverse childhood memories. Our lives are rather straightforward when we're kids. We follow instructions, go to the places we are supposed to go, eat the foods we are supposed to consume, go to school, attend practices, and complete our assignments. You see what I mean. Children, understandably, don't worry about the cards life has dealt them; instead, they simply react and flow with the situation. They are not prepared to bear that responsibility. They must evolve and expand in a variety of ways. The difficulties in life don't become apparent to us until we are older, more mature, and more independent. This is another time when many of us begin to feel assaulted or overpowered. We are always engaged in an uphill struggle, and to some of us, it sometimes feels as though we are losing that struggle. You are not, however, alone, so relax. No matter what stage or level of life we are in, this is a common emotion for most people. It all comes down to one battle: the one we have with ourselves. All the financial strain we experience, all the tension, stress, and back-and-forth, all the grind and hard work, all the pressure to provide.

That's right, we aren't fighting with our jobs, homes, automobiles, weight, families, debt, and other things. We are simply battling who we are right now against who we aspire to be, period. Strive to achieve your goals if you want to be a successful businessperson or lady. Make an effort to be the best stay-at-home parent you can be. Just remember that you are the only obstacle that will get in your way. Fight for who you want to be, and keep fighting for it. Let's be honest for a second: You might never achieve your goals, but as long as you are working toward them, you can never fail. For instance, I've always wished I could play football professionally. That ideal never materialized for me, evolving from a childhood fantasy to collegiate accomplishments. I wasn't lazy or unmotivated; life simply chose a different course for me, and I couldn't be happier. Each of us makes a certain decision at a crossroads in our lives. Even though it wasn't always the path we intended to go down, we were always meant to follow that particular route. Whatever you want to call it—faith, reality, trust in a higher force, hippie nonsense—we were all put here to accomplish something. We are all here for a reason. Our mission will not be handed to us by life, though. To fulfill that goal, we must battle every day. Bruce Lee, a renowned inspirational figure, reportedly remarked, "Do not pray for an easy life. Ask for courage to get through a challenging one in prayer. Wow, take a moment to reflect on that. It is important to acknowledge that you have overcome obstacles and shaped your life rather than claiming that it has been simple. Make sure it is worthwhile to watch when you reach the conclusion and look back on how your life developed.

Don't expect anything; work for everything, if there is one thing that over two decades of competitive athletics and one year as a coach or trainer have taught me. Life will not offer you lemonade 99.9% of the time; you must make it yourself. Sometimes, life will not even provide you with lemons. I know what you're thinking: "How in the world can I make lemonade without even having lemons?" Everyone's lemonade is unique, and that's the trick. There are numerous lemonade recipes. With the available components, you must create the finest possible lemonade. The recipe will be changed, and the result will vary each time. The lemonade you drank last year is not the same this year. Even your lemonade from yesterday isn't the same as what you have today.

We are always moving, adapting, and engaged in conflict and competition. We never visit the same place twice. We now have to decide whether to go ahead or backward. Are you today going to be better or worse than you are tomorrow? There is always conflict. We are affected by a wide range of life events, from significant life milestones to the pursuit of ambitions to the smallest day-to-day activities.

In athletics, we are taught to practice hard, train wisely, and train for the unexpected.

We are also taught not to underestimate our opponents.

So why don't we apply the same principles to ourselves? We are, after all, the only ones against us. We are the only ones who can prevent us from achieving pleasure and prosperity. Don't let someone beat you; instead, strive to improve yourself via continued training, combat, and competition. Do not ascribe labels to your accomplishments, disregard advice from others, and, most importantly, never quit! To become the best version of yourself, use the events you have in life as stepping stones. Make the most of each opportunity and seize the day. Do not give up. Never acquiesce.

Although life is challenging, the path is clear: just keep battling. You are the opponent. Be successful.

Make a conscious effort to give yourself a wonderful existence. Make changes where they are required and determine what is and is not working. YOU live this life. Be deliberate about it!

www.ingramcontent.com/pod-product-compliance
Lightning Source LLC
Chambersburg PA
CBHW071942120726
48001CB00005B/2007